Praying with the Dominicans

DOMINIC

Firm as his bronze
he is moving forward
agile and serene
through Languedoc
the world
and time
to praise
to bless
to preach
gripping the Gospel
to his heart,
with joy his answer
to the malice of a guide
who leads the way
through the thorns.

At the foundry
where the bronze was cast
a workman said:
"We, too, have to walk
through thorns."

Thomas McGlynn

Bronze statue of St. Dominic sculpted by Thomas McGlynn, OP, 1974

Other Books in This Series

PRAYING WITH THE BENEDICTINES
A Window on the Cloister

Guerric DeBona, OSB

Praying with the Dominicans

To Praise, to Bless, to Preach

John Vidmar, OP

FOREWORD BY
Maureen Sullivan, OP

Paulist Press
New York/Mahwah, NJ

Cover art by Sr. Mary of the Compassion, OP, Monastery of the Perpetual Rosary, Union City, NJ

For a list of acknowledgments and permissions, see p. 77

Cover and book design by Lynn Else

Copyright © 2008 by the Province of St. Joseph

All rights reserved. No part of this book may be reproduced or transmitted in any form or by any means, electronic or mechanical, including photocopying, recording, or by any information storage and retrieval system without permission in writing from the Publisher.

Library of Congress Cataloging-in-Publication Data

Vidmar, John.
    Praying with the Dominicans : to praise, to bless, to preach / John Vidmar ; foreword by Maureen Sullivan.
       p. cm.
    Includes bibliographical references.
    ISBN 978-0-8091-4480-8 (alk. paper)
    1. Dominicans—Spiritual life. 2. Prayer—Catholic Church. I. Title.
    BX3503.V53 2008
    255'.2—dc22
                                              2007034430

Published by Paulist Press
997 Macarthur Boulevard
Mahwah, New Jersey 07430

www.paulistpress.com

Printed and bound in the
United States of America

I would like to dedicate this book
to the Dominican missionaries in East Africa,
and especially to the memory
of Fr. Tom Heath, OP (1920–2005)

Contents

Foreword by *Maureen Sullivan, OP*
ix

Introduction
1

Blessings
5

Prayer
11

The Mass and the Sacraments
23

The Substance of Our Prayer
31

Dominican Life
45

Living in Christ
61

Sources and Further Reading
73

Acknowledgments and Permissions
77

Foreword

To pray is to engage in a distinctively human activity. We are the only beings who can transcend the physical world and entertain the possibility of a metaphysical world, a realm beyond the empirical. Theologian Karl Rahner referred to this as humanity's "transcendental capacity," a unique openness whereby we can be receptive to the revelation of God. The history of theology, based on the study of Scripture and Tradition, reveals a very basic theological principle: we have been made by God, for God. Once we are convinced of this principle, it is fair to say that coming to an understanding of the role of prayer in our lives is central to the divine-human relationship.

In exploring the concept of prayer in the Christian tradition, one is overwhelmed by the incredible riches discovered in our history: the unique Franciscan, Benedictine, Carmelite, Trappist spiritualities, the Spiritual Exercises of St. Ignatius—so many ways to approach the Divine Mystery. Each emphasizes particular aspects of the Good News of Jesus Christ. *Praying with the Dominicans* tells the story of the Dominican way of prayer and spirituality, which is grounded in the call to be a preacher, someone whose life is called to image the original preacher of the Good News, Jesus Christ.

In the pages to follow, we discover the central themes of Dominican prayer and spirituality: meditation, contemplation, communal recitation of the Liturgy of the Hours, and devotion to the Eucharist. We also find a deep devotion to Mary. From about the fifteenth century onward, praying the Rosary has been associated with the Dominican Order. A respect for the role of study is another distinctive feature of Dominican life. This is intimately connected with the Dominican motto: "To contemplate and give to others the fruit of your contemplation."

One of the central purposes for the founding of the Dominican Order was to address the Albigensian heresy in the late twelfth century. This misconception of the Christian story espoused dualism, a belief that all physical reality was evil. St. Dominic believed that creation was essentially good because God is the Creator. His approach in combating this heresy was effective then and holds a remedy for the twenty-first century as well. Dominic did not use coercion. He did not rely on ecclesiastical authority to prove the rightness of his position. Rather, he provided a practical theology to instill an appreciation for the true Christian story. Dominic believed that if his preaching was intellectually sound, he could persuade his audience; he could bring them to the truth. Given that today we live in a world that insists on reasons to believe, Dominic's approach might be more meaningful than ever.

In keeping with his incarnational approach—the principle that the goodness of human physicality is grounded in the goodness of Jesus' own real humanity—Dominic advocated praying with our whole being, soul and body. Hence, we find the use of many physical gestures in Dominican prayer—bowing, kneeling, moving in procession. For Dominic, the whole person is engaged in worship. As Timothy Radcliffe notes in his discussion of the Ave Maria: "Each *Ave Maria* suggests the individual journey that each of us must make, from birth to death....It is an amazingly physical prayer. It is marked by the inevitable corporeal drama of every human body, which is born and must die." This is Dominican incarnational theology at its best.

St. Irenaeus once commented that the glory of God is found in the human person truly alive. Were I not already a Dominican, after reading this book I would want to be one. The various Dominican prayers and customs found in these pages offer us a way of praying that is truly alive, a spirituality that is grounded in its past but so very open to its future. It reveals the remarkable divine invitation and the very human response. In *Praying with the Dominicans* John Vidmar shows consistently that St. Dominic offers followers a unique way to approach the Divine Mystery. As stated in *The Fundamental Constitution*, which expresses the basic vision of the Dominicans: "It is an apostolic life in the full sense of the word, from which preaching and teaching ought to issue from an abundance of contemplation."

Maureen Sullivan, OP
May 2007

Introduction

You cannot speak of praying with the Dominicans, or with any religious order, for that matter, until you talk about why they came into existence. About the year AD 1200, Dominic de Guzmán from Spain saw a need for a new, almost revolutionary, form of religious life. While traveling through southern France with his bishop, Diego, he was shocked at the extent of a new heresy and realized that little was being done to counter the obviously misguided ideas of these Cathars (or Albigensians, as they were called), who taught that the physical world was an evil one and was created by a malevolent God or force. Anything in this world, including human beings, was necessarily evil to the core. Marriage, physical pleasures (including art and music), and even sacraments were shunned because of their physicality. This posed a threat not merely to the church, but to society as well.

Traditional monastic orders were not prepared to meet the challenge of these new heretical groups. Benedictines, Carthusians, and Cistercians could be found in remote river valleys and distant countrysides, far away from the rising cities and towns where the Albigensians prospered. Parish priests were poorly equipped to address the theological opinions put forward by the heretics, and the clergy generally were fair game for the charges of high living, laxity, and ignorance. Dominic saw immediately that something needed to be done, and he and Diego began preaching not only about the errors of the Albigensians, but also about the hope and joy in God's creation and in the gospel message.

Dominic was essentially preaching that created things are good because God made them. In the book of Genesis we read, "God looked on what he had made and called it good." Everything in Dominican prayer-life and theology would stem from this simple belief. While the Albigensians promoted the ethereal and sometimes elusive Gospel according to John, Dominic wanted his men to preach the down-to-earth Gospel according to Matthew, which begins with the birth of Christ in Bethlehem.

Dominic realized that he and Bishop Diego, who died in 1207, would not be enough by themselves to stem the tide of this misplaced religious enthusiasm. How to do this was not immediately evident to Dominic. The first group Dominic seems to have attracted were former Albigensian women, many of whom were celibate because of their previous adherence to Albigensianism. Still filled with religious fervor, but disenchanted with the Albigensian insistence on the evil of created things, they looked to Dominic for guidance. He established a convent for them in Prouille, France, in 1206, several years before he established any houses of men, with the intention of giving their religious enthusiasm a positive direction. The establishment of Dominican nuns would prove to be a beautiful marriage of mutual support over the centuries.

But what to do with the men? Dominic wanted, at first, to establish a house of preachers in Toulouse, France; however, this began to look like just another religious order. In 1216 he obtained official permission from Rome to begin the order, now called the Order of Preachers, at the same time Francis of Assisi received permission to begin his order. (It is thought that the two founders met in Rome at this time.)

When Dominic returned to the Toulouse house in the following year, he stunned the community by announcing that he was going to disband the brethren and send them off in pairs to preach the Gospel.

Some of the brethren balked at this and one, famously, refused to leave until he had been given more money. The rest traveled far and wide, establishing houses in Poland, Germany, Scandinavia, Palestine, Italy, Spain, France, and the British Isles. It is extraordinary to see how far and how quickly these Dominicans spread. When Dominic died in 1221 at the age of fifty-two, there were twenty priories and three hundred Dominican men. By 1300, there were 20,000 friars and 141 monasteries of Dominican nuns.

Dominic's approach was to blend traditional monastic practices with mobility, democracy, and a centralized governing structure. This would prove to be a revolution in religious life and a daring attempt to meet the demands of the time. That this "system" still works today, after eight hundred years, is a testimony to Dominic's organizational genius.

But the Dominicans were not simply an "organization" or a new form of government of "friars," as they would now be called. They brought with them a certain focus and direction that centered around preaching. They would live as strictly as the heretics did—in complete poverty—and they would preach in the same itinerant manner as the heretics did, but with the difference that the Dominicans were going to remain clearly in the Roman Catholic fold and preach a message of adherence to the tenets of the Catholic faith. In addition, the Dominicans championed certain devotions—most notably those to the Eucharist, to the Rosary, and to the Holy Name of Jesus—from an early date.

This book is an attempt to share the wealth of Dominican prayer and reflection over the last eight hundred years. What St. Dominic envisioned in 1200 still has relevance for the church today—not only for the men and women who are members of the Order, but also for the average Christian seeking to find his or her way to the tremendous richness of Jesus Christ.

Blessings

A Dominican Blessing

May God the Father bless us,
May God the Son heal us,
May the Holy Spirit enlighten us and give us eyes to see with,
> Ears to hear with,
> And hands to do the work of God with,
> Feet to walk with,
> And a mouth to preach the word of salvation with,
> And the angel of peace to watch over us and lead us
> > at last,
> By our Lord's gift, to the kingdom.

—Thirteenth Century

A Blessing before Meals

This is the traditional blessing before meals in Dominican houses.

The eyes of all creatures look to you, O Lord,
and you give them their food in due season.
You open wide your hands
and satisfy the hunger of every living thing.
Glory be to the Father, and to the Son, and to the
> Holy Spirit,
As it was in the beginning, is now, and ever shall be,
> world without end.
May the Lord and giver of all things bless the food and
> drink of his servants.
Amen.

A Blessing of Rosaries

The priest wears a white stole and says:

> V. Our help is in the name of the Lord.
>
> **R. Who made heaven and earth.**
>
> V. The Lord be with you.
>
> **R. And also with you.**

Let us pray: To the honor and glory of Mary, the Virgin Mother of God, in memory of the mysteries of the life, death, and resurrection of our Lord, the same Jesus Christ, may this crown of the most Holy Rosary be blessed + and sanctified + in the name of the Father +, and of the Son, and of the Holy Spirit. Amen.

He sprinkles the rosaries with holy water.

De Profundis

The De Profundis *(Psalm 130) and its concluding prayer are said every evening in commemoration of deceased Dominicans. The prior leads and the community responds:*

Out of the depths I cry to you, O Lord; Lord, hear my voice!
    Let your ears be attentive to my voice in supplication:
If you, O Lord, mark iniquities, Lord, who can stand?
    But with you is forgiveness, that you may be revered.
I trust in the Lord; my soul trusts in His word:
    My soul waits for the Lord, more than sentinels wait
        for the dawn.
More than sentinels wait for the dawn, let Israel wait for
    the Lord,
    For with the Lord is kindness and with Him is
        plenteous redemption:

And He will redeem Israel from all its iniquities.
> Eternal rest grant unto them, O Lord, and let perpetual light shine upon them.

> V. From the Gates of Hell

> **R. Deliver their souls, O Lord.**

> V. The Lord be with you.

> **R. And also with you.**

Let us pray: O God, creator and redeemer of all the faithful, grant to the souls of your servants and handmaids the remission of all their sins, that they may obtain by our loving prayers the forgiveness which they have always desired. Who live and reign forever. Amen.

> V. May they rest in peace.

> **R. Amen.**

"Petition"

Beat upon Thy drum which is my heart.
Thrill upon Thy harp which is my soul.

Breathe into my throat a living song.
Place upon my lips a burning coal.

Shine into my mind its very phase.
Captivate my will to Thy high praise.

Strengthen Thou my soul to soar on high.
As an arrow plunge Thy love that I may die.

—Frances Clare, OP

Prayer

ST THOMAS AQUINAS

Dominic's Nine Ways of Prayer

Dominic believed strongly in the "physicality" of prayer. To pray was to connect with Christ not only with our minds or with our souls, but also with our whole bodies. Consequently, Dominican prayer involves physical gestures: bowing deeply at certain times, such as the recitation of the Glory Be or the prayer at the end of the Office; bowing slightly, or kneeling, such as at the "Eia ergo" of the Salve Regina; and prostrating oneself, such as in front of the cross on Good Friday. All of these are a sign of how seriously the medieval people took their God and their worship of him.

Here is a list of Dominic's Nine Ways of Prayer as described by Blessed Jordan of Saxony, who succeeded Dominic as Master of the Order of Preachers:

The First Way of Prayer. First of all, bowing humbly before the altar as if Christ, whom the altar signifies, were really and personally present and not just symbolically....

[Dominic] taught the brethren to do this whenever they passed before a crucifix showing the humiliation of Christ, so that Christ, who was so greatly humbled for us, should see us humbled before his greatness. Similarly [Dominic] told the brethren to humble themselves like this before the whole Trinity whenever the Glory be to the Father was recited solemnly. This way of prayer...was the beginning of his devotion: bowing deeply....

The Second Way of Prayer. St. Dominic also used to pray by throwing himself down on the ground, flat on his face,...and he would blush at himself and say, sometimes loudly enough for it actually to be heard, the words from the gospel, "Lord, be merciful to me, a sinner."

The Third Way of Prayer. For this reason, rising up from the ground, he used to take the discipline with an iron chain, saying, "Your discipline has set me straight towards my goal" (Ps 17:36).

The Fourth Way of Prayer. After this, St. Dominic, standing before the altar or in the Chapter Room, would fix his gaze on the Crucifix, looking intently at Christ on the cross and kneeling down over and over again...getting up and kneeling down again...like the leper in the gospel who knelt down and said, "Lord, if you will, you can make me clean" [Matt 8:2].

The Fifth Way of Prayer. Sometimes...our holy father Dominic would stand upright before the altar, not leaning on anything or supported by anything, but with his whole body standing straight up on his feet. Sometimes he would hold his hands out, open, before his breast, like an open book, and then he would stand with great reverence and devotion, as if he were reading in the presence of God....He had made his own the Lord's practice, which we read about in Luke 4:16: "Jesus went into the synagogue on the sabbath day, as he was accustomed to do, and stood up to read."

The Sixth Way of Prayer. Sometimes, as I was told by someone who had seen it, our holy father Dominic was also seen praying with his hands and arms spread out like a cross, stretching himself to the limit and standing as upright as he possibly could. This was how he prayed when God restored the boy Napoleon to life at his prayer at San Sisto in Rome....Like Elijah when he raised the widow's son, [Dominic] stretched himself out over the boy's body (1 Kgs 17:21).

He did sometimes recite, seriously, deliberately, and carefully, the texts from the Psalms which refer to this manner of praying: "I cried to you, Lord, all day long I have stretched out my hands to you" (Ps 87:10).

The Seventh Way of Prayer. [Dominic] was also often found stretching his whole body up towards heaven in prayer, like a choice arrow shot straight up from a bow. He had his hands stretched right up above his head, joined together or slightly open as if to catch something from heaven....And the holy master taught the brethren to pray like this both by his words and his example. He quoted the verses from Psalm 133:2, "At night lift up your hands to the holy place," and Psalm 140:2, "The raising of my hands like an evening sacrifice."

The Eighth Way of Prayer. After the canonical Hours and the grace which is said in common after meals, [Dominic] would go off quickly on his own to a cell or somewhere...; there he would sit down to read or pray, recollecting himself in the presence of God....[He] had a prophetic way of passing quickly from reading to prayer.

The Ninth Way of Prayer. Sometimes he went aside from his [traveling] companions or went ahead or, more often, lingered far behind; going on his own he would pray as he walked, and a fire was kindled in his meditation.

—Blessed Jordan of Saxony

One of the brethren asked Master Jordan whether it would be more useful for him to devote himself to his prayers or to apply himself to studying the bible. He replied, "Which is better, to spend your whole time drinking, or to spend your whole time eating? Surely it is best for them to take their turn, and so it is too in the other case."

—From *Lives of the Brethren*

One of the brethren asked [Master Jordan] to teach him which would be the best way for him to pray. He replied, "Good brother, do not fail to apply yourself to whatever inspires the most devotion in you. The most beneficial prayer will be the one which moves your heart in the most beneficial way."

—From *Lives of the Brethren*

There is no better way of serving the Word than by silence and by listening. If you go out of yourself, you may be certain that God will enter and fill you wholly: the greater the void, the greater the divine influx.

—Johannes Tauler, OP

My beloved, strive with all your might, with every effort of body and soul, to behold this true light, so that you may be able to return to the source where it shines in all its brightness. Long for it, pray for it, do all that you can, with all your strength you can summon. Entreat those who love God to help you. Cling to those who cling to God, so that they may draw you with them into God. May our loving God help us to attain this.

—Johannes Tauler, OP

Keep in mind these two little points: First, be truly humble, throughout your whole being, not only in mind and in outward conduct; think lowly of yourself, and see yourself honestly for what you are. And secondly, let the love you bear God be a true one; not just what is usually understood by the term, which refers only to emotions, but a love that embraces God most ardently. Such love is a far cry from what is usually meant by religious feeling, which is situated in the senses. What I mean transcends all sensible experience; it is a gazing upon God with one's entire spirit, a being drawn by love, just as a runner is drawn, or an archer, who has a single goal before his eyes. May the Blessed Trinity grant us to arrive at this inmost ground where its true image dwells.

—Johannes Tauler, OP

The whole doctrine of prayer from its practical standpoint can be summed up by saying that it is talking to God as a friend talks with a friend....First, the matter of prayer is originated by the mind out of the articles of faith, and the result is that the heart leaps up to love God in consequence, and this love itself is expressed in the simple language and silences of friendship.

—Conrad Pepler, OP

The first act of prayer is knowledge, the second is love....I know my friends with a deep and true knowledge, and the knowledge does not remain as though separated off in some separate compartment, having no influence upon life. I know their kindness, generosity, loyalty; and this makes my love itself without any deliberate act on my part increase also very considerably. Just as, again, the more I see the beauty of a thing or a person, the more I am attracted by it....The thing or person, in consequence of the increasing evidence of its beauty, actually draws me to it....The division of mind from heart is purely artificial; they are both mere functions of the same indivisible soul, which, when it knows what is loveable, loves it by the same energy. The very appearance of beauty produces its own effect. In prayer, then, we begin by contemplating some fixed mystery or truth, and our heart then burns within us.

—Conrad Pepler, OP

Prayer is not an abstract science or art, but a handicraft of life. It is no use for me to set out in order, however elaborately, article after article of belief: the Medievals said: "God taketh not delight in logic"—that is, there is no prayer, no union with God, in merely tabulating our knowledge of Him and describing it accurately, and remembering it in great detail. All that would be possible without prayer; prayer means that the heart, too, has been touched. It is not prayer, therefore, when I merely weave theological patterns out of the truth of faith; but it is prayer when, contemplating God as revealed to me, I find Him to be so loveable that my heart longs for His company and the return of His sympathy.

—Conrad Pepler, OP

Should We Pray Only to God?

Prayer is offered to a person in two ways: first, to be fulfilled by [God]; secondly, to be fulfilled through him. In the first way we offer prayer only to God because all our prayers ought to be directed to gaining grace and glory which God alone can give. As the Psalmist says, *The Lord will give grace and glory (Ps 83:12)*. But in the second way we offer prayer to the angels and saints, not that through them God may know our petition, but rather that our prayers might be effective through their prayers and merits. Hence it is written *that the smoke of the incense,* namely the prayers of the saints, *ascended up before God (Rev 8:4).* This is also clear from the style in which the Church prays, since we beseech the Trinity to have mercy on us, but the saints to pray for us.

—St. Thomas Aquinas

Religion is work, and it is a proverb that those who will not work cannot genuinely pray....God is in His commands, and He has bade us to work for others; and though we must retire to pray, let us not desert to pray. Christ's admonition that we should do all things spiritual, yet not leave the material necessities unfulfilled, renders the religious life a closely mosaicked labor of exalted observance and diligent work. A good religious very nearly accomplishes the impossible by the help of a miraculous Master.

—Mother Alphonse, OP

Born Rose Hawthorne, Mother Alphonse was the daughter of Nathaniel Hawthorne and the foundress of the Dominican Sisters of the Sick Poor.

Trust in God

The famous actress Helen Hayes was performing in a play at Catholic University under the direction of Fr. Gilbert Hartke, OP, the founder of the School of Speech and Drama, and she recalled the moments before opening night:

We were called up on stage by Father Hartke, and I thought, "Oh, dear, here comes that pep talk, that lecture on what to do and how not to do it." We gathered. And waited. And then Father said quite gently and quietly, "We're going to have a few moments of prayer." Well, that was something new to this old trouper, and it had a phenomenal effect. Gone were the nerves. Gone were the butterflies in the stomach. Gone were the terrors of what might go wrong. Strength flowed in, and ever after that I have prayed before an opening night.

—From Mary Jo Santo Pietro, *Father Hartke*

From a Thirteenth-Century Friar Living in Twentieth-Century London

Prayer, like generalship, must sometimes be daring. To ask a king for a trifle is to insult him. The thief daringly asked Jesus to give him the Kingdom of Heaven—to give it in a moment—and to give it after a life of sin. And it was given him, even as he prayed.

I had rather you know how to pray than that you know the definition of prayer.

Definition of Prayer: An act of the virtue of religion whereby we acknowledge that God is the Maker and Mover of all things, void of all the imperfections and limitations of created things, and infinitely perfect in Being and Attributes.

※

[God] is the First of All Beings—the Infinite Truth, Beauty, Goodness, Power. Every effort of the Finite to recognize this or to be united with it is prayer.

※

Self-knowledge is, in truth, the first step towards wisdom; yet it takes us but a little way, and takes us into darkness. To know God is the second and better truth that leads us into light.

※

The Divisions of Prayer:
The Prayer of Simple Wonderment or Reverence,
The Prayer of Praise,
The Prayer of Thanksgiving,
And the Prayer of Petition.

※

It is not so much God who stands in need of being asked, as we who stand in need of asking.

※

The true criterion of a good meditation is not the meditation itself, but the duties and trials that come after meditation.

※

He who has sent the message has sent the means.

—Vincent McNabb, OP

Prayer is the voice of desire.

—St. Thomas Aquinas

We ought to say, not that we determine to keep by Him, but only that we can determine to open our eyes to His presence, for we are kept by Him whether we will or no.

—Bede Jarrett, OP

Faith of its very nature involves an incompleteness on the part of the subject, namely that the believer does not see what he believes....In so far as the light is not shared completely, the unfulfillment of the mind is not completely overcome, and so the pondering movement in the mind goes on restlessly....To ponder with assent is, then, distinctive of the believer; this is how his act of belief is set off from all other acts of the mind concerned with the true or the false.

—St. Thomas Aquinas

The first sin in man's history was the proud determination to dominate; and now we have dominated to such purpose that we can and perhaps will destroy everything, including ourselves. If we think of love as domination we shall never know love; if we think of morality as domination, as a self-achieved self-mastery, we shall never know holiness; if we think of progress as the domination of Nature we shall never know happiness. Intellect—scientific, analytical, practical—has been abused, has been developed and idolized at the expense of the psyche as a whole; if we are to return to sanity it must be through the return of intellect to its fundamental purposes, to wonder, adoration, vision, wisdom, all of which can spring only from humility and *inwardness*.

—Gerald Vann, OP

When we get to the bottom of things, reaching their very essence with our minds, what we find is the inscrutable mystery of God's creative act....Really to know something is to find ourselves tipped headlong into a wonder far surpassing mere curiosity.

—Simon Tugwell, OP

Prayer to [the Blessed Mother] can lift us above these troubles. That is the business of prayer. We do not pray to our Lady to call attention to ourselves, [or] to call her attention to us. We do not say our Rosary in order that we may remind her that we exist. What we say our Rosary for is to remind ourselves that she exists. Prayer is lifting up, not pulling down. It is not pulling God down to my will; it is lifting my will up to God—that is prayer. It is not to make God agree with me, but to make me agree with God's dealings with me.

—Bede Jarrett, OP

Jubilee Prayer

Jubilee Prayer for the eight-hundredth anniversary (in 2006) of the first monastery of Dominican Nuns in Prouille, France

God of Mercy, in your eternal Wisdom, you called your servant Dominic to set off on a journey of faith as itinerant pilgrim and preacher of grace. With your Word of gentle Truth in his heart and on his lips, Dominic invited the first sisters and brothers to join him in a life of contemplative obedience in the service of holy preaching.

As we commemorate this Jubilee, we ask you to breathe the Spirit of the risen Christ once again into our hearts and minds. Re-create us, so that we might faithfully and joyfully proclaim the gospel of peace, through the same Christ, our Lord. Amen

Mary, Mother of the Word Made Flesh, pray for us.

The Mass and the Sacraments

ST CATHERINE of SIENA

O Sacrum Convivium

This is prayed at the beginning of the Dominican Office every day. The Latin text was frequently set to music, most familiarly by Tomas Luis de Victoria (ca. 1548–1611).

O Sacred Banquet, in which Christ becomes our food, the memory of his Passion is celebrated, the soul is filled with grace, and a pledge of future glory is given to us.

V. You gave them bread from heaven

R. Containing every blessing.

Let us pray: O God, in this wonderful sacrament you have left us a memorial of your Passion. Help us, we beg you, so to reverence the sacred mysteries of your body and blood that we may constantly feel in our lives the effects of your redemption. Who live and reign forever. Amen.

—Attributed to St. Thomas Aquinas

Two Hymns for Benediction

Tantum ergo Sacramentum	Down in adoration falling,
Veneremur cernui:	Lo, the sacred Host we hail;
Et antiquum documentum	Lo, o'er ancient forms departing
Novo cedat ritui:	Newer rites of grace prevail;
Praestet fides supplementum	Faith for all defects supplying
Sensuum defectui.	Where the feeble senses fail.

Genitori, Genitoque	To the everlasting Father,
Laus et jubilatio,	And the Son who reigns on high,
Salus, honor, virtus quoque	With the Holy Ghost proceeding
Sit et benedictio:	Forth from each eternally,
Procedenti ab utroque	Be salvation, honor, blessing,
Compar sit laudatio. Amen.	Might, and endless majesty. Amen.

—Attributed to St. Thomas Aquinas

O Salutaris Hostia	O Saving Victim, opening wide
Quae caeli pandis ostium,	The gate of heaven to us below!
Bella premunt hostilia,	Our foes press on from every side:
Da robur, fer auxilium.	Your aid supply, your strength bestow.
Uni trinoque Domino	To your great name be endless praise,
Sit sempiterna gloria	Immortal Godhead, one in three;
Qui vitam sine termino	Oh, grant us endless length of days
Nobis donet in patria. Amen.	In our true native land with thee. Amen.

—Attributed to St. Thomas Aquinas

Your mercy is life-giving. It is the light in which both the upright and sinners discover your goodness. Your mercy shines forth in your saints in the height of heaven. And if I turn to earth, your mercy is everywhere....I see your mercy pressing you to give us even more when you leave yourself with us as food to strengthen our weakness, so that we forgetful fools should be forever reminded of your goodness. Every day you give us this food, showing us yourself in the sacrament of the altar within the mystic body of holy Church. And what has done this? Your mercy.

—St. Catherine of Siena

The Sacrifice of the Mass

The sacraments are arranged round this wonderful sacrifice as the setting round the gem; Baptism prepares us for our part in it; Confirmation strengthens us in our belief in it; Confession makes us worthy of it; Holy Orders ensures for us the continuation of it; Matrimony, says St. Paul, is the symbol of it; the Last Anointing imparts to us its fruits. For it are our churches built. It is the centre of their construction, it unifies all their architectural lines. Without it the most splendid places of worship seem empty and cold, and with it, however poorly or badly they may appear, they are made alive. Our faith, our ceremonies, our lives are grouped round this supreme act of worship.

—Conrad Pepler, OP

St. Thomas [Aquinas] wanted to recover what was in essence the body of Christ itself: the sanctified body of the Son of Man which had become a miraculous medium between heaven and earth. And he wanted the body, and all its senses, because he believed, rightly or wrongly, that it was a Christian thing. It might be a humbler or homelier thing than the Platonic mind; that is why it was Christian. St. Thomas was, if you will, taking the lower road when he walked in the footsteps of Aristotle. So was God, when He worked in the workshop of Joseph.

—G. K. Chesterton

Prayer before Mass

Almighty and ever-living God,
I approach the sacrament of your only-begotten Son, our
    Lord Jesus Christ.
I come sick to the doctor of life,
unclean to the fountain of mercy,
blind to the radiance of eternal light,
and poor and needy to the Lord of heaven and earth.
Lord, in your great generosity,
heal my sickness, wash away my defilement,
enlighten my blindness, enrich my poverty,
and clothe my nakedness.
May I receive the bread of angels,
the King of kings and Lord of lords,
with humble reverence, with the purity and faith,
the repentance and love, and the determined purpose
that will help to bring me to salvation.
May I receive the sacrament of the Lord's body and blood,
and its reality and power.
Kind God,
may I receive the body of your only begotten Son, our Lord
    Jesus Christ,
born from the womb of the Virgin Mary,
and so be received into his mystical body
and numbered among his members.
Loving Father,
as on my earthly pilgrimage
I now receive your beloved Son
under the veil of a sacrament,
may I one day see him face to face in glory,
who lives and reigns with you for ever.
Amen.

—St. Thomas Aquinas

Because human beings are essentially embodied and social, grace as the spiritual mystery at the heart of reality has to be manifested in concrete, historical, visible ways. God's presence is mediated in and through creation and human history, but that mystery remains hidden and untapped unless it is brought to word. The proclamation of the word and the celebration of the sacraments (Augustine's "visible words") bring the depth dimension of reality—grace—to recognition and thus effective power.

—Mary Catherine Hilkert, OP

In every sacrament there is what is called an outward sign, which represents the inward effect on the soul, but also does actually produce that effect. Thus in Baptism the water, chosen because it shows the purpose of the sacrament in cleansing from sin, itself through the merits of Christ's passion causes the grace to operate on the soul. Again, in Confirmation the oil hallowed by the Bishop, by its being applied to the forehead, works in this way also upon the soul, conferring upon it the gift of strength....Now to many outside the Church it seems to be a difficulty to suppose that matter can so affect the spirit, yet is it not one of the commonest principles of God's dealing? Especially since the Incarnation, He has often made use of the body or the visible appearance of things to show and to cause His works on earth. In the miracles of the New Testament how often He made use of clay or water or the outstretching of a hand, or nails or spear or a cross....The whole tendency of Christian worship and doctrine is to make use of visible things to produce invisible effects.

—Conrad Pepler, OP

The Substance of Our Prayer

God's Love

God speaks to Catherine of Siena:
"The eye cannot see, nor the tongue tell, nor can the heart imagine how many paths and methods I have, solely for love and to lead them [my servants] back to grace so that my truth may be realized in them."

—St. Catherine of Siena

O immeasurably tender love! Who would not be set afire with such love? What heart could keep from breaking? You, deep well of charity, it seems you are so madly in love with your creatures that you could not live without us! Yet you are our God, and have no need of us. Your greatness is no greater for our well-being, nor are you harmed by any harm that comes to us, for you are supreme eternal Goodness. What could move you to such mercy? Neither duty nor any need you have of us…but only love!

—St. Catherine of Siena

We cannot live without reason. Science can tell us much about things that we need to know; philosophy can tell us much that we need to know still more. But of itself all this knowledge is a having, not a being; it will not by itself satisfy the hunger of the heart; it will not of itself make us whole. It will not reveal to us the heart of things.

—Gerald Vann, OP

Christ Our Light

"Christ-Light"

O Christ-Light, Christ-Light, Holy Child,
Much brighter far than Christmas Star
On that first wondrous Christmas night
When shepherds knelt in pure delight.

We are Your Christmas candles, Lord;
Light us with love, we beg of You
That we may shine to all the world.
Come fill our hearts with joy anew.

O Lord of Light, be with us still
Through all our days, through all our years,
Through times of joy and times of tears,
Our dreams, our hopes, dear Child, fulfill

That we may keep three precious lights:
The light of Faith, the light of sight,
The light of our God-given mind,
Three gracious gifts, O Lord most kind.

So kindle in us, Lord of Light,
Your flame of love, Your kindness true.
May all we love be loved by You
Especially on this holy night.

—Sr. Maryanna, OP

The Dominican *Exsultet*

The Exsultet *is the proclamation of the Easter mystery—that Christ is risen from the dead—sung at the Easter Vigil. The Dominican Exsultet differs from the Roman one in that it is more explicitly "earthy." For example, the mention of the bees who make the wax for the Paschal Candle is unique to this Exsultet.*

Rejoice now, you angels of heaven; the sacred mysteries are alive with joy.
Sound you the trumpet of salvation; sound the victory of so great a king.
And you, O earth, you too be filled with joy as you are filled with light.
There shines upon you now the splendor of an immortal king.
Look up and see, the darkness of your night is past.
And to you, our mother the Church, I also call: Rejoice!
For His brilliance has adorned you with a robe of light.
Let all the people make this temple ring with joy!
And so you also, my brothers, you stand with me bathed in the brightness of this holy light: Let all of us together invoke the mercy of almighty God.
It has pleased Him to number me, however undeserving, among the ranks of his own Levites.
Let it be Him then who makes perfect my praise of this new flame by pouring into me the luminous power of His light.
And this we pray through Jesus Christ, our Lord, His Son, who lives and reigns together with Him and with the Holy Spirit, One God, unto the ages of eternity. Amen.

V. The Lord be with you.

R. And also with you.

V. Lift up your hearts.

R. We lift them up to the Lord.

V. Let us give thanks to the Lord our God.

R. It is right to give Him thanks and praise.

My brothers, it is truly fitting that we should link together mind and heart and voice and so employ each portion of our beings in the praise of God: God the unseen and almighty Father, God the only-begotten Son, who is Jesus Christ our Lord, God the Holy Spirit.

For Christ has paid the debt of Adam, standing in our place before the eternal Father, and with his sacred blood has washed away the ancient writing in the book of guilt.

For these are the paschal mysteries, the feast of that foreshadowed Lamb who is now slain, whose holy blood adorns the doors of those who believe in Him.

This is the night, O Lord, the ancient night, on which you led them out of Egypt, the children of Israel, our Fathers, bringing them dry-shod through the midst of the Red Sea.

This night it is that burned away the shadows of sin with a shining pillar of fire.

This is the night which now in every place delivers all who believe in Christ from the vices of this world and the darkness of sin, restores them to grace, and makes them partners in holiness.

This night it is on which Christ burst the chains of death and rose up out of hell victorious.

For it meant nothing to be born, my brothers, unless we could also be redeemed. O Lord, how marvelously far your goodness to us has taken you!

How far beyond all measure is your love!

To buy back a slave, it is your Son that you have given over.

O indispensable sin of Adam, for Christ would not have died unless to put an end to you!

O happy fault, to have required so great, so good a Redeemer!
O truly blessed night, alone of all nights, to have known the hour and the time when Christ rose from the dead!
This is the night of which it was written: And the night shall shine as the day, my light shall the night become.
And so it is that the holy power of this night pardons our crimes, washes away our sins, brings back innocence to the fallen, and joy to those who weep.
It puts all enmity to flight, unites all hearts, and tempers the justice of rulers.
On this sacred night, therefore, receive, holy Father, the flame of this evening sacrifice.
The holy Church presents it to you by the hands of your ministers in the solemn offering of this candle of wax, the work of bees.
Now we know the excellence of this pillar, which the glowing fire enkindles to the glory of God.
Although divided into parts, it suffers no loss from its light being borrowed.
For it is nourished by the melting wax, which the parent bee produced for the substance of this precious lamp.
O truly blessed night, despoiling ancient Egypt that Israel might gain!
A night in which heaven is joined to earth and man is reconciled with God!
Therefore, O Lord, we pray you that this candle, consecrated to your honor, may burn without wavering to dissipate the darkness of this night.
May its flame rise up as a sweet-smelling oblation, may it burn in the company of the torches of heaven, and may the morning star find it burning still, that star which knows no setting, that star which rose up from the regions of the dead, to fill man with the brightness of His light.
We implore you, therefore, O Lord, to grant a time of peace during these paschal mysteries, and to rule, govern and

preserve with all your constant protection, your servants and all the clergy, and your faithful people, and our Bishop ____.
Look also upon those who govern us.
Through the unspeakable gift of your goodness and mercy, guide their thoughts towards justice and peace.
When their toils are over on earth, may they and all your people come at last to their heavenly home.
And this we pray through Jesus Christ, our Lord, your Son, who lives and reigns together with you and with the Holy Spirit, One God, unto the ages of eternity.
Amen.

Our Lady

The Rosary

The foremost prayer to the Virgin in the Western Church is the Rosary, in which a sequence of prayers, called a "decade," is recited while meditating on an event in the life of Christ. Each decade is made up of one Our Father, ten Hail Marys, and a Glory Be, and there are five decades in each Rosary. The counting of these prayers is facilitated by the use of beads; the word bead *comes from the Old Saxon word* bede, *meaning "prayer."*

The events of Christ's life are called mysteries, which are grouped into similar themes. So a complete Rosary might be spent meditating on sorrowful events in Christ's life, or joyful events. Following are the different groups of events, or mysteries, and the days on which they are to be remembered, according to the revisions of Pope John Paul II.

The Joyful Mysteries: (1) The Annunciation, (2) The Visitation, (3) The Nativity of Our Lord, (4) The Presentation of Our Lord in the Temple, (5) The Finding of Our Lord in the Temple. Prayed on Mondays and Saturdays.

The Sorrowful Mysteries: (1) The Agony in the Garden, (2) The Scourging at the Pillar, (3) The Crowning with Thorns, (4) Christ Carries the Cross, (5) Christ Dies on the Cross. Prayed on Tuesdays and Fridays.

The Glorious Mysteries: (1) The Resurrection, (2) The Ascension, (3) The Descent of the Holy Spirit, (4) The Assumption of Our Lady, (5) The Crowning of Mary as Queen of Heaven. Prayed on Wednesdays and Sundays.

The Luminous Mysteries: (1) The Baptism of Our Lord, (2) The Wedding Feast at Cana, (3) The Proclamation of the Kingdom of God, (4) The Transfiguration, (5) The Last Supper. Prayed on Thursdays.

Dominicans are required to recite five decades of the Rosary every day. They begin the Rosary in a way that differs slightly from the traditional, eliminating the introductory prayers of the Apostles' Creed, Our Father, and three Hail Marys, and substituting the following introduction:

> V. Hail Mary, full of grace, the Lord is with thee.
>
> **R. Blessed art thou among women and blessed is the fruit of thy womb, Jesus.**
>
> V. O Lord, open my lips.
>
> **R. And my mouth will proclaim your praise.**
>
> V. O God, come to my assistance.
>
> **R. O Lord, make haste to help me. Glory be...**

The first mystery begins at this point. The rest of the Rosary is the same as above.

So often we think of prayer as the effort that we make to talk to God. Prayer can look like the struggle to reach up to a distant God. Does he even hear us? But this simple prayer [the Hail Mary] reminds us that this is not so. We do not break the silence. When we speak we are responding to a word spoken to us. We are taken into a conversation that has already begun without us. The angel proclaims God's word. And this creates a space in which we can speak in turn: "Holy Mary, Mother of God."

—Timothy Radcliffe, OP

Salve Regina

Dominicans in the thirteenth century began a custom of ending the day with the singing of the Salve Regina, or "Hail Holy Queen," to which they also added a procession. It was in honor of their dead, and a reminder that all of us will die one day. This custom soon spread throughout the church and is still the proper ending for Night Prayer:

Hail Holy Queen, Mother of Mercy,
Hail Our Life, Our Sweetness, and Our Hope.
To thee do we cry, poor banished children of Eve,
To thee do we send up our sighs,
Mourning and weeping in this vale of tears.
Turn then, Most Gracious Advocate,
Thine eyes of mercy toward us
And, after this our exile,
Show unto us the blessed fruit of thy womb, Jesus.
O Clement, O Loving, O Sweet Virgin Mary.

There are different musical settings of the Salve Regina, with the Roman Gregorian Chant being the most popular. The Dominican version given here is more elaborate.

SALVE Dominican

Sal-ve, Regí- na, mater mi-sericórdi- æ. Ví- ta, dul-cé- do et spes nostra, sal- ve. Ad te clamá-mus éxsu-les fí-li- i He-væ. Ad te suspirá- mus geméntes et flen-tes in hac lacrimá-rum val- le. E-ja ergo, advocá- ta nostra, illos tu- os mise-ri-cór- des óculos ad nos convér- te. Et Jesum, benedí-ctum fructum ventris tu- i, no-bis post hoc exsí-li- um o-sténde. O cle- mens, o pi- a, o dulcis Virgo Marí- a, T. P. Al- le- lú- ja.

Each *Ave Maria* suggests the individual journey that each of us must make, from birth to death. It is marked by the biological rhythm of each human life. It mentions the only three moments of our lives which we can know with absolute certainty: that we are born, that we live now, and that we shall die. It starts with the beginning of every human life, a conception in the womb. It situates us now, as we ask for Mary's prayers. It looks forward to death, our death. It is an amazingly physical prayer. It is marked by the inevitable corporeal drama of every human body, which is born and must die.

—Timothy Radcliffe, OP

"Maid Mary"

You are the Lily of Israel
    And you are Sharon's Rose,
Tower of Ivory, House of Gold,
    As everybody knows.
We hail you the Queen of Heaven,
    We name you the Priceless Pearl,
But I love to picture you, Morning Star,
    As just a little girl.
A little girl in robe of blue,
    With tiny sandalled feet,
With wind-blown hair and sun-kissed cheeks,
    And a smile both shy and sweet;
Whose calm white brow unfurrowed
    Was by any pain or care;
Of Bethlehem and Calvary
    As yet all unaware.
A gentle, joyous little maid
    Who every springtime knew
Just where, beyond the Temple walls,
    The bluest violets grew;

Who watched the birdlings try to fly
    And laughed to hear them sing;
Who loved the furry woodland folk,
    Each timid little thing.
You are the Seat of Wisdom
    And the Mother Undefiled,
You are the Vessel of Honor,
    But once you were a little child.
Queen of the Prophets and Patriarchs,
    Will you refuse me aid
If in my heart I enthrone you
    Just as a little maid?

—Sr. Maryanna, OP

Hail, Holy Queen

His Mother, our Queen, we hail her. You hear it, the appeal to the Mother? Let it be your appeal too. Ask her, in the name of the Son she begot, that she would give us greater goodness, increase our holiness, such as God has already given us, that she would increase that. All the grace she had was from him. Through him she was full of grace. He did that for her. *He* did it. "He that is mighty has done great things for me, and holy is his name."

—Bede Jarrett, OP

Dominican Life

ST ALBERT THE GREAT

Preaching

He who never ceases to make his church fruitful through new offspring wishes to make these modern times the equal of former days and to spread the Catholic faith. So he inspired you with a holy desire to embrace poverty, profess the regular life and commit yourselves to the proclamation of the word of God, preaching everywhere the name of our Lord Jesus Christ.

—Pope Honorius III in a letter to St. Dominic, January 18, 1221

We do our best to live of one accord the common life, observing faithfully the evangelical counsels, fervent in prayer and in the common celebration of the liturgy, especially the Eucharist and the divine office, diligent in study and constant in regular observance. Not only do these things contribute to the glory of God and our sanctification, they also bear directly on the salvation of humankind, since together they prepare and impel us to preach; they give our preaching its character, and, in turn, are influenced by it. The life of the order comprises a synthesis of these elements, inseparably interconnected, harmoniously balanced and mutually enriching. It is an apostolic life in the full sense of the word, from which preaching and teaching ought to issue from an abundance of contemplation.

—*The Fundamental Constitution*

Preaching announces that God has defeated the power of sin and death in the resurrection, but this good news is also a call to repentance and conversion. Christian conversion always involves a twofold movement: the turn toward God (which is also a turn toward the human community, toward all of creation, and toward one's own deepest truth) and the turn away from sin (from living as "people of the lie," as less than fully human). The final word of the preaching event is not a word of judgment, however; nor does the preacher leave the community in a state of temporary awe and amazement. Rather, preaching is an invitation to follow; it is a word of hope rooted in God's promise. Preachers announce a word of life that empowers the conversion it demands.

—Mary Catherine Hilkert, OP

The mystery of preaching is at once the proclamation of God's word and the naming of grace in human experience.

—Mary Catherine Hilkert, OP

Neither tradition nor the Bible may be isolated. Assuredly God could, by His almighty power, have caused the truth to be conserved in the Church without the gift of inspired writings. But nothing prevents us from admiring the means His wisdom did choose. Tradition is like running water; it follows a regulated course only when it is contained within banks. These banks are, together with the assistance of the Holy Spirit, the written word of God.

—Marie-Joseph Lagrange, OP

Study

A Blessing before Study

O eternal Trinity, our supreme love, and true light, enlighten us. You, Who are Wisdom itself, grant us wisdom. You, Who are Omnipotent, give us strength. Dispel our darkness we beseech You, that we may know You perfectly, Who are Truth itself, and follow You in simplicity and sincerity of heart.

—St. Catherine of Siena

Before Study

Ineffable Creator, Who, from the treasures of Your wisdom, has established three hierarchies of angels, has arrayed them in marvelous order above the fiery heavens, and has marshaled the regions of the universe with such artful skill. You are proclaimed the true font of light and wisdom, and the primal origin raised high beyond all things. Pour forth a ray of Your brightness into the darkened places of my mind; disperse from my soul the twofold darkness into which I was born: sin and ignorance. You make eloquent the tongues of infants; refine my speech and pour forth upon my lips the goodness of Your blessing. Grant to me keenness of mind, capacity to remember, skill in learning, subtlety to interpret, and eloquence in speech. May You guide the beginning of my work, direct its progress, and bring it to completion. You Who are true God and true man, Who live and reign, world without end. Amen.

—St. Thomas Aquinas

"The Child Speaks"

Teacher, lead me up the path that I
Must go. Point out the way and show me
All the wonders of the world: each leaf,
Each raindrop, every flake of snow.
But, oh, my teacher, show me most how
I must think and dream and sing and grow.

—Sr. Maryanna, OP

Study

Do you want to do intellectual work? Begin by creating within you a zone of silence, a habit of recollection, a will to renunciation and detachment which puts you entirely at the disposal of the work; acquire that state of soul unburdened by desire and self-will which is the state of grace of the intellectual worker. Without that you will do nothing, at least nothing worthwhile.

—Antonin Gilbert Sertillanges, OP

The Rule of St. Augustine

The Rule of St. Augustine, written ca. 400 by St. Augustine for his priests, was chosen by St. Dominic to be the basis for his new order. It underlines the importance of community life, vows, study, and active ministry.

The Common Life and Work

Let no one work for himself alone, all your work shall be for the common purpose, with greater zeal and more concentrated effort if each one worked for his private purpose. The Scriptures tell us: "Love is not self-seeking" (1 Cor 13:5). We understand this to mean: the common good takes precedence over the individual good, the individual good yields to the common good. Here again, you will know the extent of your progress as you enlarge your concern for the common interest instead of your own private interest; enduring love will govern all matters pertaining to the fleeting necessities of life.

Leadership

Your superior should regard himself to be fortunate as one who serves you in love, not as someone who exercises authority over you....Let him be a model of good deeds for everyone: he shall restrain the restless, cheer the fainthearted, support the weak, with patience towards all....He shall strive to be loved by you rather than feared, mindful always that he will be accountable to God for you.

Mission

Itinerancy, for us as Dominicans, asks that we be attentive to our Sisters, our brothers and sisters throughout the globe, the needs we have for our own spiritual growth, the very real needs of others, and in a special way the needs of those to whom we are sent to minister. Our ability to minister will depend upon our intellectual openness to our ideas, no matter how old we ourselves are. We will need emotional balance, too, so that fear of the unknown does not preclude our "taking to the road" figuratively and literally as the Spirit indicates. There is risk involved, but it is a risk that the mission of Christ and of the Order necessitates for each one of us. The words of Kaye Ashe, Prioress of the Sinsinawa Dominicans some years back, bear repeating:

> The search for self, for wisdom, for love
> For truth, for justice, for God
> Is strenuous and unending.
> We need good companions in order to persevere in it.
> In good company, in a community of conviction, the quest never loses its relevance…its urgency…its savor.

—Elizabeth Ann Schaefer, OP

We have something to do in the world. God made us for that, each of us, separate, unique. If the work we are sent to do isn't done, no one will do it; there will be something missing in the plan of God. There will be an instrument silent in his orchestra.

—Bede Jarrett, OP

A Letter to Sisters and Associates

Pope John Paul II has set aside the Feast of the Presentation on February 2 [2003] as the "World Day of Consecrated Life." Calling attention to religious life is gratifying to all of us although we need to keep in mind that all those who are baptized can be considered "consecrated" and all are called to follow the Lord Jesus according to the pathway of our life's journey. Recently the head of the International Union of Superiors General sent a letter, which included some suggestions for some worthwhile reflections for us all.

ARE WE:
Living in mission, with Christ and like Christ?…Or just
    working?

Being a disciple of Jesus Christ?...Or being just an activist?
Discerning the movement of the Spirit?...Or following the latest fad?
Living life as an adventure of love?...Or tolerating it as a series of burdens?
Contributing to a renewed image of religious life?...Or helping only to fragment further apostolic religious life in our time?
Being happy?...Or remaining unhappy and perpetually dissatisfied?
Discovering the "New" in a life lived in the Spirit?...Or simply trying to "invent" the new?

May we celebrate this "World Day of Consecrated Life" in a thoughtful way, prayerfully considering our vocation as Dominicans. God has been generous with all of us and with the Dominican Order.

Sincerely in Dominic and Catherine,
—Sr. Elizabeth Ann Schaefer, OP

Poverty

The poor live in the vestibule of God's palace; no one can see the Lord without first seeing His servants. For eighteen centuries we have been trying to drive them away from the doors of our churches, but they always come back. They are there to teach us something, and they hold in their hands the key of the sanctuary.

—Jean-Baptiste-Henri Dominique Lacordaire

The poor keep Our Lord present on earth for us to serve. Without them, we should not know how to put our devotion to Him in practice. And it is by the giving or the refusing of this devotion that we are saved or damned.

Pie-Raymond Régamey, OP

Saints

O Lumen

The Dominican prayer day always ends with this song in honor of Saint Dominic.

O Light of the Church,
Teacher of Truth,
Rose of Patience,
Ivory of Chastity,
You freely poured forth the waters of wisdom:
Preacher of grace, unite us with the blessed.

A Prayer to St. Dominic

O wonderful hope, which you gave to those who wept for
 you at the hour of your death, promising, after your
 departure, to be helpful to your brethren.
Fulfill, O father, what you have said, and help us by your
 prayers.
You who shone illustrious by so many miracles, wrought
 on the bodies of the sick, bring us the help of Christ
 to heal our sick souls.

—Hymn, *"O Spem Miram"*

O LUMEN

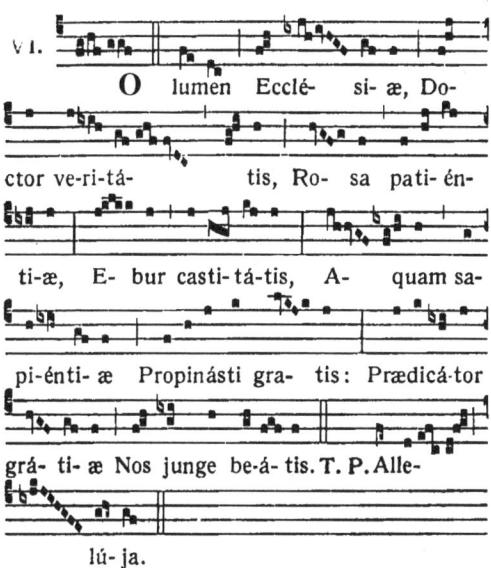

O lumen Ecclésiæ, Doctor veritátis, Rosa patiéntiæ, Ebur castitátis, Aquam sapiéntiæ Propinásti gratis: Prædicátor grátiæ Nos junge beátis. T. P. Allelúja.

Remembering Our Father Dominic

I have come to light a fire on the earth, and what will I, but that it be kindled? (Luke 12:49)

This is how it is with families, when the father is gone from them.
They miss him most at times he loved; they feel him present in the things he cherished...
They bring their memories and they think on him.
They come together, and they speak of him...

My father was a walking man.
His feet were often bleeding from too little resting, and from going barefoot,
Gospel-shod, on roads where, 'til he came, Good News had never trod.
I will remember him, walking...

My father was a talking man.
And they were burning words he spoke to those who listened.
His eyes would spark from fire in his heart 'til he could talk a single word: to God or of Him.
He talked of this, and nothing more.
I still can hear him—talking.

My father was a thinking man.
His mind was lit with thoughts too bright to hold inside him.
And his thinking was a torch to light the thoughts of minds around him.
My father's face would *glow* the Truth for other souls to know.
He was a quiet man.

My father was a laughing man.
His burning eyes were merry as they shone and looked around at all there was to do.
He flashed a father's smile and sang his way into the hearts of empty men,
To touch their souls and give them holy joy again.
No one who laughed with him left empty.

My father was a dreaming man.
He saw beyond the roads he walked on or the times he traveled in.
His deeper self beheld him visions that his fearless will would grasp for certainty.
He planned for other souls, and rooted all his dreams in his fidelity.
I never saw him sleeping…

My father was a praying man.
His every conversation, day and night, was heart with
 Heart—spoken with one voice and one delight.
My father's self was always bowed before his God in
 prayer.
He took his only resting there.
His silent cell was all the world.

My father was a weeping man.
The tears that washed his manly cheeks had drenched his
 gentle soul and flowed,
In unembarrassed waves, to flood the sin-parched days of
 worldly ways
Too dry to know their thirst.
I've heard him sob when other men were sleeping.

My father was a building man.
His hands were rough and calloused and his back was bent
 from bearing weights and burdens.
My father built a house to last beyond his time;
He put his plan in its design and in its first foundation.
He spent himself in building.

My father was a dying man.
He perished every day.
My father walked and laughed; he talked, and sang,
 and cried;
He lived with lifted arms before the Crucified.
He pleaded there for sinners' souls—and all the while,
 he died.

—Sr. Marian, OP

God had given Dominic a special grace to weep for sinners and for the afflicted and oppressed; he bore their distress in the inmost shrine of his compassion, and the warm sympathy he felt for them in his heart spilled over in the tears which flowed from his eyes.

—Blessed Jordan of Saxony

Saint Albert the Great

God our Father, you endowed St. Albert with the talent
of combining human wisdom with divine faith.
Keep us true to his teachings
that the advance of human knowledge
may deepen our knowledge and love of you.
Grant this through our Lord Jesus Christ, your Son,
who lives and reigns with you and the Holy Spirit,
one God, forever and ever.
Amen.

Saint Thomas Aquinas

If we were to call [St. Thomas Aquinas] a philosopher, we would be saying very little. If we were to call him a theologian, what we are saying is too vague. If we call him a man of prayer whose prayer-life was centered around the Eucharistic presence of our Lord in the midst of His people, then we are getting close to the heart of that extraordinary life.

—Ferrando Minnogio

Saint Martin de Porres

Loving God, Martin's charity not only embraced the needy women and men of his time but even the animals of the field. Help us to be instruments of change in our world being mindful of Your Son in the face of the poor. Grant this through the same Christ our Lord. Amen.

It is the saints who are independent; they have mastered themselves and are whole; they do what they like and no man can stop them, for they laugh at terror and torture, having nothing to lose. It is the saints who have power; they need not rely on bribery or blackmail or bayonets, for their power is really theirs, within them, and it is simply by being themselves that they sway the world. When the lions lick the feet of Paulinus in the Roman arena, when Laurence makes fun of himself on the gridiron [he said, "You can turn me over, I'm done on this side"], when thousands flock to the confessional of the illiterate Cure of Ars, when millions love and honour Bernadette because she was humble, when people lose their hearts to the saints not for what they do but for what they are, because in themselves they are real, in themselves they are lovely—that is power. Real power is like real happiness: you find it when you have stopped looking for it because you have found something even more important to do.

—Gerald Vann, OP

LIVING IN CHRIST

Virtues

I must beware of making purely negative resolutions, for then I shall simply look back at the past as measured by failure. If I make up my mind to avoid this or that, the result will be that I shall have no other standard of judgment in moments of spiritual stock-taking than the occasions on which I have broken my resolutions; the final result of this will be that I shall exclaim in disgust that I had better never have made any resolutions at all—a perfectly logical conclusion. The more cheerful and helpful way is to reverse this procedure. Already I have found out what my predominant fault is, for I have made a thorough and careful examination of conscience. Then when I am certain, or at least as certain as I can be, I must concentrate not on the sin, but on the corresponding virtue. My resolutions now will not be to avoid this or that, but to increase or develop this or that. I shall not finally measure my past by a series of faults, but by the number of times, few perhaps but none the less real, when I have actually managed to achieve success. The gardener who spent all his time digging up the weeds and never thought very much of strengthening his plants would produce a very tidy but depressing garden....So in my soul all my energies should first be spent upon encouraging my poor feeble virtues to grow strong, and then by their very strength they will cause the sins to diminish.

—Conrad Pepler, OP

There are two ways of keeping God's word, namely, one whereby we store in our memory what we hear, and the other whereby we put into practice what we have heard (and none will deny that the latter is more commendable inasmuch as it is better to sow grain than to store it in the barn).

—Blessed Jordan of Saxony

One cannot share with others what one does not have in oneself.

—St. Catherine of Siena

Those who do not love God, do not know how good He is.

—St. Rose of Lima

My work is of very little value in itself, so I try to enhance its worth by giving it the merit of obedience.

—St. Rose of Lima

Contemplata aliis tradere
"Hand on to others the fruits of one's contemplation."

—The motto of the Dominican Order

God speaks to Catherine of Siena:
"No virtue can have life in it except from charity, and charity is nursed and mothered by humility. You will find humility in the knowledge of yourself when you see that even your own existence comes not from yourself but from me, for I loved you before you came into being."

—St. Catherine of Siena

O high eternal goodness of God! Who am I, wretched as I am, that you, high eternal Father, have revealed to me your truth and the hidden snares of the devil and the delusion of selfishness I and others can be subject to in this pilgrim life, so that we might not be deceived either by the devil or by ourselves? What moved you to this? Love. For you loved me without being loved by me. O fire of love! Thanks, thanks to you, eternal Father.

—St. Catherine of Siena

The more [the soul] possesses you the more she seeks you, and the more she seeks you and desires you the more she finds and enjoys you, high eternal fire, abyss of charity.

—St. Catherine of Siena

We should speak of good or evil in human actions in the way we speak of them in natural things; when an act has the fullness of being it should have, it is good; otherwise, it is evil.

—Thomas Chrysostom O'Brien

What matters most is not what one does, but the love with which one does it.

—Jordan Aumann, OP

All evil is the result of mistaking means for ends.

—St. Thomas Aquinas

Progress is essentially moral. The prizes of life are less for men of genius than for men of character.

—Vincent McNabb, OP

That God is object means that the acts of faith, hope and love exist and are what they are because God communicates Himself as the one to be believed, to be hoped in and to be loved in return.

—Thomas Chrysostom O'Brien

Nothing has been told us by God as a matter for remembrance; it is committed to us to become a means to achieve the higher life.

—Bede Jarrett, OP

Faith is viewed essentially as the initiation of personal union with God, in which man in his whole person responds to God....Faith is not bestowed to provide a theoretical world view; it is the beginning of salvation. God does not address man in faith in order to provide him with information, but with the invitation to salvation. *Credere in Deum* indicates that belief is part of the loving response to a loving God, of a person to a person.

—Thomas Chrysostom O'Brien

Real power is to the lover. That is why it is idle to hope or work for a new world, a league of nations, unless we are ready or at least trying to be ready to kiss the leper: not the priest or the levite but only the Samaritan can rebuild the world.

—Gerald Vann, OP

It is *being* that comes first in importance; and Christian morality tells us first of all not what we should do, but what we should be.

—Gerald Vann, OP

In the beginning God planted a garden. He is Lover and Creator; and He made man in His own image, to be lover and maker in his turn. There is evil in the world and so the garden is no longer given; we have to conquer thorns and thistles and make the garden before we can begin it and keep it; but it is still our destiny to be gardeners, and to be gardeners for God.

—Gerald Vann, OP

> Behold, my children, the heritage I leave you: have Charity for one another, guard Humility, make your treasure out of voluntary Poverty.
>
> —St. Dominic's Last Will and Testament

Discipleship

> I am Yours, and I desire to belong to You alone. I will be eternally faithful to You, and I desire to lay down my life for You.
>
> —St. Rose of Lima

Friendship

This was Fr. Thomas Heath's favorite of all the poems he had written.

Dogwood reaching through the trees
Delicate, white and Japanese,
Stepping faintly through the green
Of the smoking wet ravine,
Is something like a prayer for grace
Rising from an anxious place,
Is something like your presence when
The heart is lowland, scrub and fen.

—Fr. Thomas Heath, OP

Fr. Thomas Richard Heath, OP, a native of Massachusetts, was the first vicar provincial of the Vicariate of Eastern Africa. He spent the last eight years of his life serving the people of Kenya. He was beaten by robbers in January 2005 and died a few days later, age eighty-five. This book is dedicated to him in particular, as well as to all Dominican missionaries in East Africa.

Contrition and Forgiveness

The Dominican Confiteor

I confess to almighty God, to blessed Mary ever virgin, to blessed Dominic our father, to all the saints and to you brethren, that I have sinned exceedingly by thought, word, deed, and omission, through my fault: I beseech you to pray for me.

—From the Dominican Rite

It is the mercy of God which alone can bring me to my knees and make me ask for my forgiveness; and this mercy I must regard as a high privilege, something which adds to and in no way lessens the value of human dignity. On Him must my eyes be fixed so that even my sins are remembered, not for my own humiliation, but for His tender love. I go to seek His mercy, not simply because I love Him, but far more because He loves me; not because to err is human, but because to forgive is Divine.

—Conrad Pepler, OP

"Lenten Thoughts"

Dear Lord, what have You done for me?
My heart bleeds at the memory
Of blindfold, buffet, mockery,
Of pain endured so willingly,
That Heaven's Gate might opened be.
For me You suffered injury;
For me You climbed to Calvary;
For me You died upon the Tree.

Dear Lord, what can I do for You?
How shall I prove my heart's love true?

My past ingratitude I rue;
This Lent, Lord, I will start anew.
With holy thoughts my heart imbue;
Make all my words and actions, too,
My sacrifices small and few,
A pledge of gratitude to You.
—Sr. Maryanna, OP

Suffering

Mark well how in the Gospel, when the Lord promised that he would render a hundredfold, he added, But with tribulations; wherefore we must never for a moment allow ourselves to forget that if we would receive a hundredfold we must be prepared equally to suffer tribulation. Yet shall the time come when the Lord shall repay us no longer a hundredfold but with infinitude, when no tribulation shall any longer come to you, but together we shall drink of the pure and unmixed chalice of everlasting joy. Meanwhile we must wait patiently, accepting comfort with humility and tribulation with courage, and finding both the comfort and the strength in God's Son Jesus Christ, who rules over all things, blessed for ever and ever. Amen.

—Blessed Jordan of Saxony

God speaks to Catherine of Siena:
"I have shown you, dearest daughter, that in this life guilt is not atoned for by any suffering simply as suffering, but rather by suffering borne with desire, love, and contrition of heart. The value is not in the suffering but in the soul's desire. Likewise, neither desire nor any other virtue has value or life except through my only-begotten Son, Christ crucified, since the soul has drawn love from him and

in virtue follows his footsteps. In this way and in no other is suffering of value."

—St. Catherine of Siena

"Mourning Song"

There are three ways to mourn, the wise men say:
First with our tears upspringing in the heart,
Whether we think or speak or rest or pray,
Unbidden they with stinging pain will start.

Then there is silence, silence in the mind;
We cannot bear to verbalize our loss.
Compared to what we've lost and cannot find
All else in this sad world seems so much dross.

The highest form, surprisingly, is song.
When we can lift our spirit to the skies,
The separation seems indeed not wrong,
As God's grace helps us fully realize.

Wherefore, dear one, your rest, your joy I sing,
And pay my debt to you, remembering.

—Sr. Maryanna, OP

Thanksgiving

Prayer after Communion

Lord, Father all-powerful and ever-living God,
I thank you,
for even though I am a sinner, your unprofitable servant,
not because of my worth but in the kindness of your mercy,
you have fed me

with the precious body and blood of your Son, our Lord
 Jesus Christ.
I pray that this holy communion
may not bring me condemnation and punishment
but forgiveness and salvation.
May it be a helmet of faith
and a shield of good will.
May it purify me from evil ways
and put an end to my evil passions.
May it bring me charity and patience,
humility and obedience,
and growth in the power to do good.
May it be my strong defense
against all my enemies, visible and invisible,
and the perfect calming of all my evil impulses,
bodily and spiritual.
May it unite me more closely to you,
the one true God,
and lead me safely through death
to everlasting happiness with you.
And I pray that you will lead me, a sinner,
to the banquet where you,
with your Son and Holy Spirit,
are true and perfect light,
total fulfillment, everlasting joy,
gladness without end,
and perfect happiness to your saints.
Grant this through Christ our Lord.
Amen.

—St. Thomas Aquinas

Thanksgiving for Little Things

The good we are to be thankful for need not be big things in themselves, but there is nothing to stop us putting an infinite value on them if that is the impulse of the heart.

The slightest thing can light up our whole life in joy, thanks, service, praise, for we always see it as a mark of God's goodness. Gratitude is called forth by the kindnesses we receive and spurs us to return those kindnesses. It tends always to make us give more than we get, and to give it in a different way....However material the blessing we have been given, Gratitude never sees its material value, but only the good will behind it, which is beyond all valuation; it answers by giving our whole soul. It bursts out in the utterly generous praise of the Gloria in Excelsis: "We give thee thanks, O God, for thy great glory"—if we get nothing by it, it is enough that You exist, and that You are splendour itself, for us to glow with gratitude.

—Pie-Raymond Régamey, OP

Sources and Further Reading

Sources

Catherine of Siena. *Catherine of Siena: The Dialogue.* Translated by Suzanne Noffke, OP. Mahwah, NJ: Paulist Press, 1980.

Chesterton, G. K. *Saint Thomas Aquinas.* New York: Sheed and Ward, 1933.

Early Dominicans: Selected Writings. Edited by Simon Tugwell, OP. Mahwah, NJ: Paulist Press, 1982.

Hilkert, Mary Catherine, OP. *Naming Grace: Preaching and the Sacramental Imagination.* New York: Continuum, 1997.

Jarrett, Bede, OP. *Bede Jarrett Anthology.* Edited by Jordan Aumann, OP. Dubuque, IA: Priory Press, 1961.

Lagrange, Marie-Joseph, OP. *The Meaning of Christianity According to Luther and His Followers in Germany.* New York: Longmans, Green and Co., 1920.

Lathrop, Rose Hawthorne. *Rose Hawthorne Lathrop: Selected Writings.* Edited by Diana Culbertson, OP. Mahwah, NJ: Paulist Press, 1993.

McNabb, Vincent, OP. *Oxford Conferences on Prayer.* London: B. Herder, 1902.

Pepler, Conrad, OP. *Sacramental Prayer.* St. Louis: Herder, 1959.

Régamey, Pie-Raymond, OP. *Poverty.* New York: Sheed and Ward, 1950.

Sertillanges, Antonin Gilbert, OP. *The Intellectual Life.* Westminster, MD: The Newman Press, 1959.

Tauler, Johannes. *Johannes Tauler: Sermons.* Translated by Maria Shrady. Mahwah, NJ: Paulist Press, 1985.

Tugwell, Simon, OP. *Reflections on the Beatitudes.* London: Darton, Longman and Todd, 1979.

———. *The Way of the Preacher.* London: Darton, Longman and Todd, 1979.

———. *Ways of Imperfection: An Exploration of Christian Spirituality.* Springfield, IL, Templegate Publishers, 1985.

Vann, Gerald, OP. *The Seven Swords.* New York: Sheed and Ward, 1953.

———. *To Heaven with Diana.* Summit, NJ: Dominican Nuns of the Perpetual Rosary, 2006.

———. *The Water and the Fire.* New York: Sheed and Ward, 1953.

Vann, Gerald, OP, and P. K. Meagher, OP. *The Temptations of Christ.* New York: Sheed and Ward, 1957.

Further Reading

Anderson, Robert, and Johann Moser, trans. and eds. *Devoutly I Adore Thee: The Prayers and Hymns of St. Thomas Aquinas.* Manchester, NH: Sophia Institute Press, 1993.

Bedouelle, Guy, OP. *St. Dominic: The Grace of the Word.* San Francisco: Ignatius Press, 1987.

———. *In the Image of St. Dominic: Nine Portraits of Dominican Life.* San Francisco: Ignatius Press, 1994.

Hinnebusch, William, OP. *Dominican Spirituality: Principles and Practice.* Washington, DC: The Thomist Press, 1964. This great historian of the Dominican Order writes an insightful look into the Order's spirituality.

Jarrett, Bede, OP. The *Life of St. Dominic*. London: Burns, Oates & Washbourne, Ltd., 1934. This short biography captures the spirit of St. Dominic better than any other.

Murray, Paul, OP. *The New Wine of Dominican Spirituality: A Drink Called Happiness*. New York: Burns & Oates, 2006.

Pieper, Joseph. *Guide to Thomas Aquinas*. New York: Octagon Books, 1982. This short classic is a brilliant introduction to the world of St. Thomas Aquinas and the first Dominicans.

Vicaire, M-H. *Saint Dominic and His Times*. Green Bay, WI: Alt Publishing Co., 1964.

Acknowledgments and Permissions

Paulist Press would like to thank the following for permission to reproduce material to which they hold the rights:

Rev. Benedict Croell, OP, and the Dominican Friars of Eastern Africa, for permission to reproduce the photograph of Fr. Tom Heath, OP, on the dedication page. Web address: frtomskids.org.

The English translation of the Opening Prayer for St. Albert and for the Prayers before and after Mass by St. Thomas Aquinas from *The Roman Missal* © 1973, International Committee on English in the Liturgy, Inc. (ICEL). All rights reserved.

Rev. Joseph Barranger, OP, Prior of the Dominican House of Studies, Washington, DC, for the painting by Sr. Mary of the Compassion, OP, used on the cover.

Rev. Ambrose McAlister, OP, trustee of the McGlynn estate, for the photograph of the statue by Rev. Thomas McGlynn, OP, and the poem by Fr. McGlynn on the half-title page.

Sr. Marie of the Precious Blood, OP, for "Petition" by Sr. Frances Clare, OP.

Sr. Ann Marie, OP, Prioress General of the Nashville Dominican Sisters, for "Dominic Our Father" by Sr. Marian Sartain, OP.

Sr. Mary Ann Wiesemann-Mills, OP, Prioress of the Sisters of St. Dominic of Akron, Ohio, for permission to include the reflection by Sr. Elizabeth Ann Schaefer.

Sr. Mary Grace, OP, of Corpus Christi Monastery, Bronx, New York, for her drawings on the part-title pages.

Sr. Anne Kilbride, Prioress of the Columbus, Ohio, Dominicans (Congregation of St. Mary of the Springs), for "Christ-Light" (p. 34), "Maid Mary" (p. 42), "The Child Speaks" (p. 50), "Lenten Thoughts" (p. 68), and "Mourning Song" (p. 70) by Sr. Maryanna, OP.